VIA FOLIOS 99

I Stop Waiting for You

Poems

Mary Jo Bona

BORDIGHERA PRESS

Library of Congress Control Number: 2014944618

COVER ART: "Drawn Curtain" by Christine Perri

The author and publisher thank Patricia A. Rangel for her kind permission for the use of "Drawn Curtain," which is part of her private collection.

Printed in the United States.

Published by
BORDIGHERA PRESS
John D. Calandra Italian American Institute
25 West 43rd Street, 17th Floor
New York, NY 10036

VIA FOLIOS 99
ISBN 978-1-59954-079-5

ACKNOWLEDGEMENTS

Grateful acknowledgment is made to the editors of the following publications where some of these poems first appeared: *From the Margin: Writings in Italian Americana; Paterson Literary Review; Unsettling America: Race and Ethnicity in Contemporary American Poetry;* and *VIA: Voices in Italian Americana.*

Missing me one place search another,
I stop somewhere waiting for you.

—Walt Whitman

For Judy, forever

TABLE OF CONTENTS

III. REMAINS

I Stop Waiting For You

I confess: I talk to you in my sleep,
when I'm most at peace with knowing
you'll never call and I'm flying
over your house admonishing in rhyme.

On the Sabbath they say He stayed home.
You're so busy making worlds
that Sunday turns into Sunday
with a blink of your steely eyes,
while I sit back praying you
haven't died, haven't lost another
maker, the one who named your trouble
on the day you ran away.

On the streets I search for someone
like you, a builder of tricky houses,
the shifty movers of my dreams.
One day after miles of running,
you'll fall asleep and you won't
recognize me in your dream:
you'll shake yourself awake.
I'll be living two-thousand
miles away with a lover very brown,
who flies with me in the day.

If you let your eyes melt a moment,
you'll know that I've turned
around seven times seventy times
and stopped, somewhere, waiting for you.

I. CROSSINGS

The Act of Remembering

To remember them now is to take them out of pain,
the overwhelming storm of their bodies.
If we forgive the death in the dying
of our loves, and we must, let us damn
the disease that savaged their vessels.
Let forgiveness overlay them with the gesture
of leaves, brown-dead and quiet.

The project now is palimpsest:
rewriting the body alive on the death quilt.
Dear, your body of old, lush and lean,
morning prose and gladioli,
recalls the lithe line of poetry:
smooth, hurting, opening up my wound,
covered over now with mute longing.

Naming your beauty, your city haunts
and wild desire, appliquéing them on my heart.
Projecting you in my walk and words,
the way I put my hand to my brow.
Constructing a panel three feet by six feet
with your name enables reparation,
makes memory and forgiveness one.

What Is Found There: NAMES 1996

Their death is built at dawn.
Our hands lay winding sheets around the grounds--
a ritual of quilts, 40,000 plus,
fabric mausoleum of those who've died.
Massive work, unfolding and re-folding
gingerly with care, our children sprawled
on wet cold grass, awaiting midday crowds,
while a woman prays the rosary on her knees,
another asks to lie down on the quilt
to measure six feet by three feet.
I tell her no, she cannot press her weight
against the frailty of hearts and cloth
and midnight rush down risky streets awash
with fierce beauty. And yes, they are the size
of coffins made with grief and pride,
with single words like Mike or Sal or Love.

Their faces always kill: their eyes beacons
in the nights, roaming streets for love.
Signatures hurt, too: the niece who writes
she loves her uncle, dead at twenty-nine;
his hands folded neatly still in death,
in peace after monstrous roaring had him
screaming like a beast. His lover cleansed
his body, delivered him from pain
dressed the temple of his youth, and bore
aloft the quilt he made with the midwife's
expertise of hands.

I am docent of the western quadrant,
surrounded by the oldest quilts, sparsest
and most plain. Dead and buried ten years and more.
Gloved hands behind my back, I am told
to watch for vagrants, vandals tearing open graves.
But what I find is nothing short of bliss,
the ecstasy of quilts, ubiquitous,
growing middle-aged, lucky, lucky they!
Soon they will be seeking a new home,
in middle America, where silence
of grasses comforts their old age,
and the deer and the antelope play.

Rough Crossing

He is barely thirty-three.
Twelve midnight and he's soaked on cotton sheets.
He turns his head, blurred eyes squint
at the pink face of his sputtering clock,
its Roman numerals black beacons
in endless night. His pleading hands
clench in prayer, trembling like the clock's
hands. He prays a midnight vigil.
Prays to God to ease the fear
of drowning in his sweat. Begs instead
for a lifeboat and keys to unlock the engine
of his pain. Every pulse throttles
his ears, his hands, and long lean legs.

His body's on fire with disease.
Four a.m. the featherbed
under his wet back feels full of malice.
He hoists onto another pillow, brief relief.
He thanks the cotton for the gift of a cool breeze.
His crazy thoughts, an anchor doomed
to deep seas. His leaden tongue and eyes
reach beyond sleep and God and love
and dreamless ease.

Dawn. He calls his twin and hears
her faraway voice better than his own.

She tries to know his kind of night
of sleepless fear. She stills him, promising

to fly that day, a ticket in her hand,
bags packed for years.
To herself, she calls him dear-heart
before departing on the plane.
She knows his body's naked on the shore.
Dear, she thinks but dares not say,
your night crossing's close,
quick sailing soon.

My Father's Sorrow

My father, with automaton intent, paints
the mailbox again, leaf-brown.
It's the wrong color for summer
and he forgets to paint the matching fixture
on the house, the light that stays on in hope
of some final retrieval of his dark-nighted soul.

We come home late, empty, and do not sleep.
At night, he waits for good news by the stoop,
anything that will tell him that his son,
who is dying, is not dying. He left
the empty nest and one unborn robin's egg
atop the outdoor lamp, a scapular
of hope. He repaints the box at dawn,
before we leave for the hospital,
drugged and wan, shells of ourselves,
our echoing the sound of a full July moon
on a night dragged into infinity by our silent howls.

Four eggs hatched two weeks ago
when there was hope. He asked me for the truth
and I said I did not know. I did what I was told
and washed my hands in the death room
the hundredth time before touching
our dying beloved's brow.

He asked me for less after that:
he said, perhaps the deep-colored thing
was not done for naught?

I told him no, it was painted like twigs
and the home feeling of the past.
And father, your son is dying
and we are watching only that.
He knew something then and his heart
became a scalpel of pure pain.

Snoqualmie Falls, July

It rained.
The mist over my eyes
looked white against mossy trees,
green, sticky with summer.
The Falls, violent in May,
soothe now in late July, bursting
from a brown socket, blooming
like rain on green rocks.

The mists, slippery as memory,
guide me toward Deception Falls,
a fuller violence, as risky as precipice.
Teetering there, I remember
dinner the night before, eating
monkfish with abalone, feeling holy
and succored by its barley and risotto
layering, imagining a menu with Southern
red sauce and Italian wine.

The fall would be brief and beautiful,
violent as blood. At the edge of a smooth
wet stone, I bring us back to the night
before when I told you I loved you.
Though one-year dead you were dying
still in my heart, the mud and leaves
clinging to my bones, sticking on my face.

I remember a longing so intense,
as irresistible as *la famiglia*,

ominous as memory. My hiker's boots
stay rooted to the rain-wet rock. I fall
back on green moss, wet branches, stumble
over a nurse log, feeding its children.
I feel your hand like mist, still,
palpable, breathing.

Out of My Closet

For Gabriella Brooke

I threw your photographs,
heedlessly in the back of my closet.
I had a plan. I refused to look
at hundreds of pictures,
from your babyhood to successive
graduations and trips
away from your prized Windy City.
I stuffed them all in an oversized K-Mart bag.

Close-mouthed, eyes and ears shut,
I went blind and deaf to the white crinkle
rubbing against my ankles. I power-walked
my way out of that bedroom,
and, over my shoulder, eyed warily the dark
doors of my closet, knowing their false closure
their accessibility, brown whores, disclosing
secrets of my prayers: that I might escape
remembering the rocky storm
that crushed your body.

Then a friend tells me over lunch
with sunlight blasting in our window,
blinding our eyes, that she had to get her brother
out of her closet. He died before there was a name
for AIDS. She planned to bury his urn in homeland
Sicily, but was family denied.
She ordered granite from Vermont
and placed her waiting name next to his in Spokane.

Months later, fists no longer closed,
breath no longer clogged, I pull out the bag
and spread your pictures all over the room.
Some in the closet, others blossoming
into the bedroom, down the hallway, in my arms—
all of them, and what I see is that smile, that smile:
it was your best-kept secret. Mine, too.

July, and the Night Is Still

I wait until midnight to talk with you.
Give you rest during the day
when everyone is feeling
your name in their mouths.
They drape beads around bashful hands
and learn holiness.
They are very beautiful, like you,
my love.
I wait until midnight to hear
your lullaby in lilting Italian,
hoping you've acquired the old
tongue, like a lover,
all at once and intense.

I talk to the house like a child,
pleading that it stay quiet,
placating the creaks.
The anointment takes hours:
the house, my body--
cleansed, starched, shined, waiting.
The woodwork has been massaged
into a softness like brown hands.
The furniture, buffed and waxed,
gets sent downstairs to make room
for the arrival I'm planning like
love.

You don't come. I'm ready to invite
any ghost to enter my house,

but my monasticism is too shrill,
too white.
Outside, the July night heat
dulls the stars that still shimmer.
On this second year of your going,
I remember you
and this house is blessed
with the silence
of your night stillness.

October summer, Spokane

Feels like summer.
Yet, the gnats congregate in bunches,
frenetically flying till dusk.
They get lodged in our throats,
when we take late day walks
before Daylight Saving Time ends.
Grey dawns in Spokane make us bear-like
by noon. We hide in offices,
or huddle under canopies lit at three.
Early darkness cloaks our already-peaked bodies,
yet our hands still yearn, cupping the sun.
October summer lays her head softly in our laps,
we bow down to meet her, half way.

Snoqualmie Falls, November

For Marie Rinaldi

The autumn mist falls from the trees,
rises unbidden in front of my eyes.
Last time I walked with him on Chicago
streets was in the midst of heat
and his dying. These November Falls
offer him no succor from a fire trapped
inside a house, fomenting furious cells.

In the whispers of autumn leaves
I walk alone and think now of another
brother, quick as fire, dashed down
on a merciful bed, a leaf-sodden track
that took him like lightning, lovely and brutal.
He was beautiful and Italian.
He drank wine with his twin, on birthdays, too.

She and I with rosary beads hung
in our minds walk city streets
and wonder about July heat and dying young.
We hike down mossy trails
and ponder cool September days,
dying alone with the oaks standing by, mourning acorns.

The bread we take to our mouths today,
Italian invocation, hosts our very mealtime.
The vapors from the mists steam our window,
overlooking the Snoqualmie Falls.
We drink wine together now,
summon and imagine.

Amazone

For Auntie Carm

Blond-haired, green-eyed, Italian girl.
The first of your 'type' to enter the Wasp
world of advertising, 1943: you were
young, healthy, and eager to be French.

(Red-headed grandfather be blessed
for lightening things up a bit, but our people
lived too far South and vowel-ending surnames
darkened our hopes for approval.)

You didn't have a daughter to teach
you how to become ethnic, and my niecehood
was spent revering your silence,
your permanence, the parfum on your dresser.

* * * * *

I like now to imagine the irony of dressing
rituals: when you swathed yourself
in Frenchness and fetched your married sister
for the opera, singing Italian arias along the way.

Before Heart Surgery

My mother cries out at 3 a.m.
Trembles from tornado winds,
flinches at house sounds.
I listen beside her in the bed:
her cry sounds like "mom,"
but I am half asleep and think
that I may be calling her, as of old.

She's grown small and feverish
from insomnia rooted in her system.
She imagines being spared from sleeplessness
is deathlike perfection. She says the house
is falling down, and the Chicken Little of her dreams
shouts at air, shakes tiny fists at menacing skies.
I tell her the house is not dying, and she is not the house.

Next morning she snaps a photo of clematis
dying on the vine and declares, "here's proof:
the plants won't take root either."
I ask her if she wants to die, let her heart strangle
her one day as she throws towels in the dryer,
an activity she performs with a somnambulist's
touch, perfunctory as rain.

"No, I thought I did," she replies next day, 4 a.m.,
when we talked till dawn. Then she slept.
She tells me midday she let the clocks go, their dinging,
chiming, ringing and whistling every quarter
hour a burden to me, while I stayed with her.

I supposed those antique clocks
kept revisiting her sleepless nights,
but she told me, before surgery,
she could feel their sound, regular as heartbeat,
smoothing her brow.

Mother's Shoes

I tell my daughter about Mother's size,
six-and-a-half double "A," the petite
black pump, the shine of indigo.
Years, I hid those shoes in my closet
waiting for my feet to grow
into them. At twenty-two, I thought
her body possessions too sacred
and serious for wearing. I was a mere girl,
with vast and airy plans.

It became a matter of living
up to daily standards, at forty,
in a stuffy home, filled with stacks
of *Better Homes and Gardens*. I spent
time organizing calendars, trying
new recipes, pleasing and pleasing
la famiglia. I wondered how Mother
had done it better, negotiating kitchen space
in a starched, hand-stitched apron
and patent-leather pumps, no less.

Now I'm old and too busy to worry
about a ghost in the closet, created
out of neediness of loss. I remember
now an exhausted Italian woman,
dying in an oxygen tent at fifty-six.
I tell my middle-aged daughter, size eight-
and-a- half "B," that Purple Hearts
no doubt found better feet for those shoes.

On Seeing Your Quilt in Auntie's Bookstore Window
Spokane, WA.

Letters emblazoned under bright light,
I wince in acknowledgement, your name,
our family secrets, so public. Your death,
like your doctor's degree, hanging on high,
this time in the window of a bookstore
you never saw. If you'd come visit me

you'd catch me looking in the mirror
at my double and know the searing
feeling at midnight on an empty downtown
street, midweek in balmy April
as I gaze at the name that's mine, too.

The blue of it, the length and width
of it: panel suspended in air, crippled bird,
bound interminably with strangers.
Grandmother would have hissed, *stranieri*,
be careful. Don't be mingling with boys
you don't know.

Oh, would you come home with me?
I am so lonely on this midnight street.
I want to drape your quilt across my shoulders
like a cape, your body's memories tattooed
on my heart. Catch me looking for you, beloved,
around this corner, under these lights,
across the city street: my eyes wave furiously.

Anniversary

I want you to know him like I did:
a blaze of fire, his body bronzed
till the day he died. I want you
to know him like that: brown, blazing fire
imminent peril within him
like long-sleeping lava, bubbling
just beneath. Doctors monitoring
internal combustion, waiting
on nature's chaos.

And my lover watching the way I say
I love him, gesture of the inconsolable,
hand against brow, wordless summons
to follow him, when his dark suffering
became unspeakable, not dignified,
not heightened humanity, but greed
that sucked the breath out of him, dragon-
blowing fire in his limbs, suffering
without metaphor.

His brow smooth as a child's after the fire
ate his lungs, burned through a mind so keen
his words were like knives in my ribs
when we were cruel and young.
His face cool alabaster in my dreams--
but on the bed at his death,
a blaze of fire, brown beauty,
and hot, so hot.

II. PASSIONS

Travel

Home space feels quiet as death.
This, after hectic travel, constant movement
in air, on shuttles, in trains and busses.
By the time I reach our home,
it's late afternoon and bright as sun against snow.
But all I feel is midnight in my blood
and movement in my bones. Every muscle
taut and twitching, and ears shuddering
from the deafening world of traffic jam.
The polyphony of voices I hear are disembodied,
like waking out of restless sleep on a plane,
hearing strange giggles in the ear.
In our home space, it's empty of you,
of music blaring, Louis Prima, Leontyne Price,
Dolly Parton, who knows what will be playing
to keep my bones warm and my ears clear
of the detritus of noisy, irksome travel
in this outside place that's become,
for all its frequent foreignness,
another kind of home.

Morning Glory

6:00 a.m. The streets are clean on the drive
home from O'Hare Airport. No remnants
of Saturday night's mayhem in sight.
The sun glistens on pavement like fragments of glass:
I imagine underneath the cement and stone,
brown earth shimmers. Chicago morning's brightness
shocks my bleary eyes and stirs memories
of walking those eight cold blocks
to the bus stop, before narcotics hit the streets
like incessant punches in the mouth.

Hoodlums congregated on street corners
near my high school, eyed the Catholic girls
in their rolled-up skirts, but never touched,
just whistled softly through spaces in their teeth.
I could wait all morning for that turtle of a Motor coach
to inch its way to my stop, and no one bothered me:
not the truckers who honked and waved,
not the blabbering woman who smelled of wet wool
and had snot on her face, not the uniformed school boys,
guffawing and harrumphing, though their well-fed bodies
scared me more than the black-eyed hoods
in their leather and boots.

Decades later, I can't imagine so short a skirt, shivering
so long in winter air. Can't imagine watching
all of them without the blurring sounds an animal
makes when it escapes the crushing tire
of a speeding car. All I remember then was the dawn
sun like glory on the coldest days.

Migration, Back East

My end-of-century migrations
take me from Chicago to Madison,
then Spokane and New York, traversing
three time zones. Landscapes
as different as deciduous and desert.

I long for my old haunt with heaviness
of spirit. A city taut with crowds,
snow-soaked alleys, the Wrigley Building
twinkling in December midday sun.
That's Chicago: town of my birth and parting.
I visit her now like a lover, all breathless
expectancy, petting the lion's paw
as I race up the steps of the Art Institute
to meet the girl with the morning lark.

Washington State began and ended with loss.
The white-tailed deer visited us on dark cold
nights, daring to cross once dirt roads, and dying
for their effort. I lost my brother
then. The air was stiff and dry,
fragrant as wine. Pine trees
loomed in space, peacefully swaying.
I smelled juniper on my useless hands.

On Eastern Standard shores,
I live three-thousand miles
from our half-empty house back west.
My lover longs to give birth to permanency.

Where to find it?
In this in-between place, we learn
to desire less, pray more.

Our momentary parting weighs
less than the granite of loss,
yet feels like death.
Our eyes fix on the threshold
of possibility, or, better: frequent talks,
hungry visits.

When We Talk

I dress in armor,
steel-plated knight garb.
But like a knight
I want to chase you down,
swoop you up.
I can't bend with all this weight,
reach the Holy Grail.
And my horse won't budge,
he nibbles dry weeds by
the frozen shore.

When you talk,
the walls rumble.
I feel shaking deep in my bones.
You encourage my weight loss,
ask questions that make me
sweat under steel.
I take off the weight
just for you,
Just for you.

You open your mouth,
flowers blossom by the shore.
I go there with you.

The water is sweet--
we share the cup.

Your Letter, Even in My Dream

Opening scene:
I watch my dreaming hands search
the letter you never sent. My reckless
hands rifle through mail boxes
at the old university where I was once
a young professor and dared to love you.

Scene shift:
I am sitting on a lawn chair in a long driveway
viewing silent films. I watch footage
of a historical past in some way mine.
Of people so poor that if luck
allowed them to grow old
they would never dare speak
except to speak of another's life.
Their shame covers them like an invisible shawl,
quieting their wounds. They are as mute
about their poverty as the blind alleyways
in Chicago before street lamps shown brazen
lights on their wooden spoons, olive oil cans,
and stale Italian bread.

Next reel:
I see an enormous claw-footed tub
and a black kettle filled again and again,
heating water for bi-weekly baths. Who had luxury
of cleanliness in a cold-water flat?
It was cold, they were exhausted,
yet managed to send monthly remittances,

care packages of clothes and hand-embroidered
handkerchiefs to homeland villages.

End scene:
Library stacks.
Easier to search archives for immigrants'
ornately-scripted letters home to the old country
than to find one from you,
even in my dream.

Morning Walk

Parched lawns dot the yellow landscape at dawn.
I feel you in the air today, a touch
like soft brown, a voice as lush as tropic
zones that bring no relief with rain. At six
a.m. I hear you through the leaves: you whisper
that the fall winds will end our tryst, as true
as autumn brings shorter days and nights,
predicting gloom and grey.

Mile two my heart steadies in its rise,
my gait's less awkward, muscles warming fast
in one-hundred degrees. Cows huddle
under shady trees with low hanging
branches whose leaves begin their turn,
though no one sees this yet. When I met
you years ago, we walked this route,
passing the lone farm surrounded by building
contracts for more and more houses.

By the time we reached mile four,
we were in another country, despite bulldozers
knocking down the old man's farmhouse,
the empty barn where children once had played.
I was perfectly in love with you then.
Now, on the road home, about mile five,
the water cascades down my shins and thighs,
I want to slide my arms into your arms--
hide from changes in our old neighborhood,
recall when we were young, *a braccetto*,
and lovers for a time.

You Must Know This

That I will overturn tables
at the French café if you so much
as narrow your eyes at the beautiful
woman ambling past us.
I'll scream, too, and call you
a whore. You will chase after me,
all arms, explaining yourself again,
but I'll read nuance in your eyes
and shoot *il malocchio* at your heart.
Before that, I'll fall to the ground,
stomach smashed against concrete,
wrists splotchy and cheek grazed
while I kick and cry.

I feel you raise your hand to your head,
pull up your hair, squeeze the back
of your neck, look around with furtive eyes
at passersby, asking not so much for their
sympathy as for their friendship.
You assume they think that you are trying
to talk sense to a crazy, high-strung
woman, with a ranting temper
and a body that raves.

I look up at you wide-eyed and wink:
next time you call me too emotional,
too Italian for my own good, watch
the show: I do spectacle for free.

Passion Kiss

That look before it happens, slight movement
of the chin, a parting of lips. Your eyes
serenely on mine, asking split-second
permission to claim my mouth.
Like falling, like pitched fever in night,
like thirst so profound the sound of water
buckles the knees. The heart and limbs
pummeled by the shock of standing upright
in front of your eyes. Now they question mine,
but my eyes hold no key and you know
how to get in anyway, are getting in now.

Your eyes have me stunned. Your hand
like a hush brushing my back as you open
the door to a house I've known before,
but to a house I shouldn't be in. My limbs
like robots march toward the entrance hall
which glitters in May. Windows and light
everywhere in this house of gold
and whites and quiet patterns on the couch,
wood floors beneath our feet. I lean
against the bright wall dazed by so much light.
And your eyes, your parting lips, your hand
against my chest, all soft pressure to say yes.

Safe Landing

A tall woman ambles into the local
Safeway, dressed in a silk suit and black
Bally pumps, shiny, new-minted coins.
It's Saturday afternoon. She feels cool
and breezy, slightly superior, wacky, out-of-place.
She watches her hands pick apples from towering
formations, perfect pyramids,
triangles of cool desire. She wants sex.
This always happens when she travels.
Dressed to the nines, she touches down
in the ordinary, wanting to strip tease
for the worker making cheese-balls
for bored shoppers. No matter, she just flew
in from giving the key-note address. No
matter, she was fêted with a literary
prize worth thousands: she imagines sex
with the stock boy, the beefy one.
Honestly, she scolds herself, she'd rather
climb her husband's thighs, a safer way.
Yet, she considers toppling the apples.
On the way out, she winks at the blonde cashier.
Perhaps the girl thinks she's being motherly.
She's not.

Gift

If I could uncurl your tiny fist,
finger by finger, lay your damp hand
on my cheek, hold you in the crook
of my neck, your lips pressed
against my rapidly beating pulse,
smooth your tangled hair that's all flyaway
in the day, hum my mother's songs,
rocking you back into soundless sleep,
so that you wake a clean sheet, purged
by dreams you do not recall.

If I could do that for you in the night:
guarantee your safety, my room next door
an anchor, the hallway light your beacon
and the strange thump in the wall that pitter-
patters when it rains, a feathery heartbeat.
Then you'd thank me some dark night
decades away as you do your own holding,
your heart pumping as you stumble
wildly out of bed, your big fists fighting
demons in the dark as you lumber toward
the room where your child's nightmare rides.

This Child between Us

Invisible as air, this child between us grows
like a gaseous balloon and hangs behind our eyes.
All night it wrestles our dreams away,
flaunts a wide-mouthed smile
before our eyes. We rescue ourselves
though silence at the kitchen table,
chamomile tea at dawn. We wonder how long
we've lived like refugees in our bed,
the place where we remembered hope,
the round space between our grownup bodies
an uninhabited universe,
wide as a berth, parched as a desert sun.

We will not have children.
Reap what you sow sounds cheap like a joke
smacked across our faces just when we line
our hands in prayer after we weep.
We renounce ourselves for selfishness,
for wanting life between us and through us.
We have now this sudden grief, realized
by our woman-love, nurtured by our febrile
nights, our wild love that was our repast
for so long, but left us with a roaring hunger.

Garden Party
A Dream Poem

I rise from the late-night table
with no words. My head sleepily
nods at the inside voices, blurred
by too much wine grown warm
beside the candlelight. My graceful,
carefree exit smooth as a trance.
I stroll around the midnight grounds,
my heals sink in spongy grass.
The dew-soaked roses closed like red
fists, I search the shed for the green
thumb who grew those fitful dreams.
I find you there, instead. Tanned, lovely.

You say nothing, but lean against the warped
door that has not closed in years. I glance
upon brown boots, thick laces climbing
up the tongue and your bare leg under
blue jeans. I come closer to your hair,
smell wild flowers, a halo of bright scent.
I smile at the thought of the blue-throated
hummingbird taking nectar from your hand,
bursting a frantic heart on a girl like you.

I let my hand glide down your face,
my mouth move noiselessly against your ear.
My other hand slips in yours. I nod my head
and glance at your good-bye. You disappear
at dawn. The inside voices of night are gone.
When dreams call, they call you and I come.

Seven Years

This pain I feel for your death
is an old friend whose balm is all voice
and hands. Pain made your eyes
close down on us, who watched
without words. I shut my eyes and hope
to feel one moment of your hands,
your voice brown velvet on my skin.

Flight Home

I want these two men to be lovers.
I sit next to them and watch askance
as the older of the two takes control
carefully like a new mother.
The beautiful younger, in baseball cap
and bright eyes laughs with the steward
when he spills the Virgin Mary on his lap.
How far apart they are in years, this couple
in love. I call the young one giddy
before my eyes return to Audre Lorde's words.

When the younger lover stands up to stretch,
I see the cap covers a head bald from treatment,
from family history, maybe both. When he walks
down the aisle to stretch some more, the man
next to me has eyes all solicitous, locked
into a love deeper than desire, nearly despair.

Later, the furious proficiency of dinner hour
over, tray-tables locked in upright position,
I get up to stretch myself. When I return
the man asks if I could tell his son about the author
of *The Cancer Journals*, the book left on my seat.
I do. I give him all her selves, poet, mother, lesbian,
activist, librarian, teacher, lover. She died
but much later, after recovery.

The young man no longer travels by himself.
Seizures from the brain cancer, his father says.

The son nods sagely, adoring this man
who travels from Michigan to New York
to accompany his son home.
The son tells me more after they switch seats.
He finished medical school, despite his pain.
He diagnosed his fatal illness, explaining
the furious pattern roiling in his brain.

I wave goodbye to them in Chicago.
The red splotch on the young man's trousers
has dried. They walk together, an elderly couple
on a winter's stroll, closely.

Gym Teacher

I reminded the athletes too much of their
army-trained fathers and roughened brothers.
I exacted order and decency
at all times, even in locker rooms where girls
are wont to gossip and giggle. I commanded
their silence and obedience, if not their respect.

The non-athletes, the majority devoted
to bubblegum and boys, gave me grief.
Always grief. I didn't mind the sick ones,
the asthmatic Italian, for instance,
who couldn't jog worth beans, but swung
on the rings like a chimpanzee. The Polish gal
failed dance, but socked the hell out of the softball
in Spring. Lazy girls incurred the punishment
of hanging on a bar against the green wall
and doing leg lifts till they cried. I watched
the brevity of their sorrow with dry eyes.

Behind my back they hissed "fucking bitch."
I was hard-hearted. My sick son's eyes
still gleam in my mind after all these years.
His pure love for all the girls. I'd roll him
in his wheelchair to the sidelines during basketball
games. How he loved the arc of that ball,
its flying zeal, he'd squeal with delight,
while the fans would hold his hands.

In gym class, they never forgave me
for what I did to the fat girl, never.
The athletes turned their heads

and shot balls, but the others hugged
the walls while I forced Margaret to clear
the horse like the rest. I expected equality
for all. When she hit her wobbly torso
and fell face first on the pad, I moved
to the next girl, as though she disappeared.

I saw out of the corner of my eye
one of the non-athletes, thin,
but no good with a ball,
shake her head and place her hand on her heart
the way my mother did when fights erupted
in a house full of men. I hated her then.

That gesture burned a mark
in my mind. Her hand betrayed
a purity like Stanley, my son,
whose love was insistent like pain.

I'd like to say those were my salad days,
when youth was not yet pummeled
into tenderness. But I was middle-aged,
saddled with a sick son, a low-paying job
at an all-girls' academy, a husband so kind
I badgered him, hoping he'd strike like my father.
How I managed the feat of a good and patient
man is a miracle only the Virgin knows.

The girl with the sorrowful hand
waves to me in the night, beckons
with words and promises
a poem about my life. She vanishes
in the day while I tend my garden
and prune those weeds out of sight.

Ten Years

I am your older sister now.
See how this works? Alive,
you'd call me a handsome woman,
gray at the temples, slightly thalasemic.
If you were still practicing, you'd care
for my health, the ache in my back,
the knob in my neck. But you are dead.

Did I tell you I can't get over this,
over you? That my feet didn't slip
from the falls because I loved the piney
air, the cool green at my feet, the sheer ease of breath?
Did I tell you I didn't want to die
so I could go on loving you?

You were just becoming a man, late twenties,
when you made the late April phone call.
Mid-afternoon silence shattered
by that call, the shaky breath of your voice.
The knowledge of your illness,
uncontrolled shaking, painful hiccoughing,
all mine, inconsolable, after your call.

What bliss could follow?
Three years to love you still,
to hear your midnight voice,
to smell your body.
To hold your hand
and manage things at the end.
To be your twin nineteen more days

after turning thirty-three.
To tell you I loved you all my life.

That Friday sun was bright on your face.
That final mid-morning hour.
Your face, still brown and young
and inexpressibly sad.
Ten years, dear-heart.
Ten years, beloved younger.
My pain is the family's, deep-boned, boundless.

III. REMAINS

Today

The air is thick with smoke,
stirred up by wind on a gauzy
late afternoon. Warm. Very warm
September. A timid sun trickles
through skies heavy with clouds.
On the way home, a woman smells
autumn seeping in her car: she opens
the windows and sun-roof, remembering
the Kennedy Expressway, one midnight
summer years ago, when seventy m.p.h. winds
whipped her hair. Her eyes blurred
by so much speed, she loved
Chicago nighttime driving
with skyscrapers silhouetted
against purple skies. Her deep-bone
love and the taste of juniper on her lips.
The blues men at Kingston Mines
reminding her of how much she missed
him today, late afternoon, September,
when autumn presses its beauty on
leaves falling gracefully like him.

Hometown, IL.

At thirty-four, mother felt bereft
of street-cars and corner stores,
houses and businesses snuggling
against each other in the city
where she was raised. She learned to drive.
She became a mother of three under five
and rose in wee hours to study physics:
how to shove the kids out the second-story
window during a fire she was sure would burn
down the house. Before dawn, her world felt desolate,
her mother buried at Mt. Carmel much too young.
The street lamps in Park Ridge too serene
and the drunkard next door missed the driveway
again. The battered tree between the houses
was cut before Dutch Elm disease attacked our street.

During summer, my brother and I traded
guppies for the angel fish, and spent hours
at Mary Ann's Pet-shop pondering guinea pigs and gerbils.
Before the small town turned into a mini-city,
empty lots dotted the landscape and prairie weeds
made my sister sneeze. No such things as fences:
our neighbors waved tiny hands in our direction,
perhaps a block away from our rust-brown
house, with a driveway long and lean,
one my father never quite mastered in reverse,
though he never hit the tree.

Sundays mother drove us to Thompson's Grocer
after Mass, where we'd buy jelly rolls

and long-johns, imagining the bakery
all through the sermon, the communion wafer
a thin prelude to the irresistible necessity
of food. Father read the *The Tribune*
through and through, while we warmed
up the T.V. for *Family Classics* and laughed
at the way Park Ridge rolled up its streets by six.

Before dinner, mother ran and shut the windows.
Father shook his head when we three jumped
and screamed out *Pupa Cu L'uova*
in Grandma's Abruzzese dialect.
Ready or not, little town, here we are.

Voices in the Dark

In Memory of Our Lady of Angels Fire, December 1, 1958, Chicago

For Grace Noverinni (1926-1985)

Trapped in the corner of your mind
the children howl. They claw
at tiny classroom windows. Stricken
by temperatures so high their hearts
stop, while firemen on low ladders grab at air.

Your daughter ran home from school
that day without her coat. Pneumonia weather,
and she walks home half-naked and shaking.
You went to retrieve that hand-me-down
at Our Lady and heard a sound
so appalling it knifed you in the night.
Frigid air snapped at your face.
Smoke bellowed out of the school.
And the children. You fell to your knees,
took small breaths after that.

Later, you heard about the nun
who led her pack of kids down the hall,
crawling on knees through black air.
Later you stood ready to run, nose sniffing
the house for gas, eyes locating exit signs
in Montgomery Wards.

In your older dreams, you told your daughter
you saved those children. Their suffering faces

became a cairn that marked a place in your mind's
eye. Not one of them was lost.

Father in a Photo at 42

All those cigarettes. Those endless drives
in the Pontiac before the expressway was built.
He was always in the wrong lane, woolgathering.
My father imagined living on a lone hill
like a monk, away from a city razing his old neighborhood
before his eyes. He rarely spoke.
We children only guessed at his grimness.
My mother buffered us from his silent sadness,
told us to sit still and *sta zitta*! *Omertà* to protect
the family against those *stranieri*, outsiders
who might hurt us.

I gaze long on his sleepy face, his cropped
salt-and-pepper head with the two of us
each straddling a leg, propped close on his lap.
Five years old. We were beautiful:
he was hopeful nothing bad would happen to us.
My father was one generation past the immigrant terror,
but one too soon to boast the permanency of protection.

We were at the fairgrounds, on Chicago-land's
favorite Ferris Wheel, but all I recall
were the snapshots from the photo-booth.
Each shot blazed forth at our star-struck eyes,
wide with the terror of delight.
Our quiet father held us close to his ears.
Next day, he yawned and smoked and drove.

Surname

The local dry cleaners can't get my surname
right: I tell them "a" as in "apple," final vowel,
but they hear "er" in their Long Island way
and take my Italian name away. Alas,

I return to thirty-plus years ago when boys
on bikes laughed hysterically like girls
as they screamed with youthful lust the name
at me down our suburban streets.

I thought it must be bad, my disgraced name.
Straightway, I sped on bike to our small-town
library. Assignment number one: search this word
on the sly, not at home where penises

were tallywackers and mostly ignored. I saw
the unabridged dictionary loftily atop a lectern.
My mouth watered. Without ado, I found the lambaste
they threw at my name, but knew it meant more

than blunder or error. Plan "B": ask brother, a boy
who knows such things. He won't tell me! Scorns
me for such unfitting concerns, an old-world
Sicilian rising up in him, boy version of *Birth of Venus*

atop her lofty conch. Older sisters are better conveyors
of learned knowledge, so willing to share
their growing store of lust and gore and good fun
watching younger sister grow in horror

that her name could be so used. My sister laughs,
teases me but faintly because it's her name,
too. She stocks my store some more when
she whispers in my ear—lez be friends—hugs me,

winks, and walks away. Somehow I know the boys
who rearranged my name made a blunder
beyond prurient play. From my sister's punning ways,
I walk away, knowing more than I'm willing to say.

Nancy M.

For Shannon and the girls at St. Scholastica Academy

I was weak and no teenage visionary.
But your body drove you to take it down.
Young as I was, I knew that much.
I barely knew you before you took the pills.
When seniors were assigned "Little Sisters,"
mine was a skinny freshman with freckles
and five sisters. She didn't need me.
You, with your bad skin, and your hair,
all frizz, a shapeless Afro.
You, with your Italian name
and burly brothers from our hometown
who wouldn't hurt a fly.
You, with your weight beyond burly.
Gravitas pulled you down.

The last time I saw you,
I passed you in the hallway,
smelled Bazooka on your breath.

Assisted Living

For Carmen E. Orlando (June 3, 1920-January 19, 2003)

Chaperoned in youth by uncles with kind eyes,
my aunt grew up. They stared but did not see
her. She primped and paraded downtown,
where the streetcars in Chicago
screeched and whined. At eighteen
she began her workaday regime, trudging
to the same firm for fifty years,
only to be escorted away at sixty eight.

Her immigrant father, bereft when he arrived,
stripped from the belfry's call, his village
beckoned in old age, though he never returned.
At seventeen he was free from everything except poverty,
and the accent marking him foreign, not assisting
him in living in the land of plenty, America the free.

Oldest child, my aunt obediently placed
the pay envelope in her mother's hand,
lived with her parents into her thirties
in the two-flat on Highland Avenue,
blessedly freed from the indigence of the war years.
Her mother placed her hand on a heart
ruined at birth from rheumatic fever
and died at fifty-six. Her father moved away.

Depression-born child, trained by want,
regimented small soldier marched downtown,
saved everything, her mother's recipes
stowed in a storage bin for forty years.

Now, in her final sickness, just beginning,
when she yet has the words to say it,
my aunt sits in a stark, clean, well-lit room.
She grieves *le vie vecchie*, the faded apartment,
her stuff shorn, depleted, weathered, thrown away.

First born, eldest sister, is confused by me
and startled by the bright ottoman.
She tells me she needs no assistance
in living. She's impatient with her hands.
They're in the way these days. I want
her to hold the gift she gave me:
her olive-pitted rosary beads from *Roma*,
hoping she'll imagine the old land
and its luscious trees. She wants none of it.
She tells me she's got the decades memorized anyway.

Long Island

On the porch I watch a brief summer
storm around dusk, lightning
far enough away, but thunder
cracking close to my ears.
And the smell: sweet, cool.

June rains differ from other months.
It's warm outdoors, not hot.
Mosquitoes haven't bloomed
like poisonous plants around the periphery
of our backyard full of trees. Wildflowers
we left spreading across the back,
kept in its natural state unlike the neighbors
with their built-in pools, their tiled patios
and manicured shrubs.

Our rhododendrons in ferocious bloom flash
explosions of early June in purple, fuchsia,
and, later, lavender fading to white. The light
starts up briefly like dawn before the rain abates
in this almost summer storm
that put the final kibosh on the late-blooming
lilac planted in a corner of our backyard:
near their fence that separates
us from their always empty pool.

Alien

Two Mexican day-laborers stand on the street-corner,
wait to be chosen by white pimps in pick-up trucks.

The man, with property and papers and money and language
asks one minor question, showy in retrospect.

Yes, they are Mexicans. So he beats
them in his basement within an inch of their lives.

In his mind, race is religion.
He prostitutes himself to the almighty creed.

And turns beet-red with blood and sweat,
only half-believing his election to punish is decreed.

The other half just punishes to feed his excitement,
like the hard-on he used to get when watching cowboys defeat
Indians.

Bathing My Mother

Prepubescent thin, my mother
asks that I not look at her when I take
her by hand to shower. I tell her
not to worry: she's so small
I barely see her. We still have laughs,
though her pain burgles her body,
stealing heft and time and quiet
on the balcony, where she once swung
on the glider. Now, back and forth ease
hurts beyond compare, but compare she
does to days of old. The swing in the two-flat
on Lawndale Ave. brought squeals
from my mother when she was a girl.
Where her mother moved them from place
to place, skirting infectious disease,
the landlord's daughter's TB and the son
who took my mom more than once to the cellar.

The kids on that block called her "No. 11,"
stick thin she was, the black and white photos
exposing a Depression youth where food
was sacred and scarce, youthful bodies trim and taut.
Her mother's cooking a largesse shared
with hobo men who sat on her back stoop
while she fed them minestrone soup and bread.
My mother learned to cry in youth. Being thin
meant being poor, but poverty was spread
like sickness across the city, men in stained fedoras
waiting in bread lines. My mother's family

lucky enough in numbers to share their food,
but not much else.

Now, my mother's sadness for her body
reminds her of the hard times she tried to forget.
Where her parents' poverty was a fleet-footed
burglar who made off with most things by day,
except for that second-story back-porch swing
and the nighttime fear of lights turned off
and bills not paid.

My Father's Letters

He is young.
He will never be more innocent.
He uses untranslatable words like "swell," "doggone," "ye-gads."
He would never sound a barbaric yawp.
He's just trying to impress my mother,
a high school student to whom he dutifully
writes for three years while he shuttles
from Fort Knox to Fort Bragg to Fort Smith
to Camp Chaffee to Fort George Meade,
and, finally, abroad, to Caserta, Cassino, Pisa
and Venice, taking furlough from the "Disciplinary
Training Center," where he works as an army guard
in 1945 Italy.

When I've become adult enough to wonder
about my father's youth, he tells me this:
the most intelligent inmate he ever spoke
with was Ezra Pound.
I nearly fall from my chair.
Later, I search scores of letters
my mother heedfully saved, ordered
and dated, for reference to the sage poet.
I find none.

Instead, I read comments like "soap, cosmetics
and cigarettes are dear luxuries" in the midst
of a ruined southern Italy. My father laments
the "pathetic looking beggars" that are Italian
street children. Their favorite song is "Pistol Packin' Mama"

and nearly all the Italian kids can sing it. My father
sends my mother the Mediterranean edition of *Yank:
The Army Weekly Newspaper*. Hungrily, I read
through it, captured by photos of rubble
in war-torn Italy.

Studded with coinages, my father's vocabulary
pleased the ear, teased the eye. These facts
I learn: that his coaxing my mother to "don a pair of slacks
and be Rosie the Riveter" bespoke a playful banter
he maintained in old age. That his gratitude
for being fed three meals
a day during the war years clung to him like sweat.
Call it immigrant fear.
Call it the inheritance of poverty,
my father frets about food every day.

But it's the begging that strikes my heart.
Begging a teenaged girl from the old neighborhood
to write him more often, scolding her when letters
do not arrive, entreating her to write soon,
or, like a pauper, he'll solicit alms on another corner.

My mother's shoebox is a beggar's purse,
appetizingly stuffed with his letters and hers.

Hearing From You, Too

For Dan Butterworth

On the other line, a man with a low dark voice
calls my name. I catch myself on the white
kitchen wall, steady my breath,
feel fire in my speechless throat.
I see instead your brown face
through the screen and the way
you would stroll in like a man
with all time in creation.
In another haven, you are haunting
me with melodies of deep sound,
brown rivers humming like infinity
so that I must read with new eyes.

But in the meantime, I've become
a spectacle of sounds--gasping, crying,
whining and keening like nails bleeding
down blackboards. I fumble with the white wall,
down, down, on knees that are humbled
by the exactitude of sound.
The man with the low, dark voice
is a friend with inspiring hands:
he clears his throat and begins again.

My Sister's Name

Praying, my mother begins reparation.
During our daily call, she offers
justification for my sister's problems
like she dispensed cod-liver oil
to us as children, with the practical hope
in healing all ills. Unready to swallow,
I tell my mother she cannot believe
the name she gave my sister caused life-long
harm. Angry now, I recall Bizet's *Carmen*,
and third-grade teacher, Sister Carmella,
and Tina De Rosa's Carmolina, flowering artist.
But then I remember Waller.
Waller Lancaster, long-ago colleague.

The shame, like an old coat, covers
my body. The hairshirt nobody sees.
Fifteen-year old memory hanging in the closet,
and for what? To tell me shame doesn't evaporate
like sweat and time, but clings like a cloak
I stowed long ago. He winced when
hearing my sister's name. Winced!
Pitied the wearer of that name.
My body burned with shame then, not rage.
Cara Carmen, *carina*.
Carmie, Carmie, *mia bella sorella*.

My mother calls today, doing penance:
"I named her Carmen. I gave her my mother,
Carmen, I gave her my sister, Carmen.

I gave her the shame I watched my mother
scrub away like the twenty stairs outside
the two-flat in Chicago. Carmie, Carmie,
mia cara figlia, forgive me my generational love,
my woman-love. My daughter, dearest."

Mothering Mom

Finally towards his life's end,
my father sleeps with one eye
open, one ear a tuning fork
honed to my mother's sounds.
As she scratched and inched
her way out of bed, my mother's hands
clutched the metal bars
of her beloved walker, embracing
her torso like a steel hug.
Her wedding bands clanked
against handles like a noon bell
calling children home for lunch.

Now the tinkling sounds
of my mother's movements
are a clarion call for my father,
who is terrified. He stays awake
for the first time in fifty-seven
years of married life.
Past crying infants in the night,
past after-dinner coffee and sleepy silence,
past napping through movies at the local theatre,
past dozing at houses of friends whose travel
slide shows brought his lids down like stones.
Past blaring televisions, phones ringing,
fighting children, long-winded adults,
neighborly chats at twilight hours
in Chicago Junes when folks seek
outdoors like fireflies at dusk.

Past all the noisy sounds of living
he closed his ears to like a penitent
fasting but not chanting, seeking peace
in the desert of a city he found in sleep.
My Dad's now haunted in waking dreams
by my mother's sounds, all in his one good ear,
and bells ringing in the deaf one.

July 24, 2011

It happened, Phil.
In New York on your anniversary.
We weren't thinking of unions
sacred or other back then,
just trying to save your life.

A Valediction: Forbidding Marriage

"'Twere profanation of our joys,
To tell the laity of our love."

—*John Donne, "A Valediction: Forbidding Mourning"*

Every Sunday you read aloud *The New York Times* marriage
announcements. Your locution is perfect.
You only read about the women.

We used to scoff at those sorry couples bidding farewell
to a certain kind of freedom. Now they look like us.

We eloped so long ago, made a house in three states,
my mom showering us with big-item gifts,

your dad sending us the ping-pong table
that survived the cross-country migration like us.

Thirty-years ago, we chose companion-in-life
to describe ourselves, until we read the obituaries

and learned "long-time companion" to the bereaved
was always gay and dead. We shifted to nicknames

on love notes in and out the door, rushing to work,
alongside shopping lists, in between separate travel.

We've come to love our steadfast engagement,
our long-married love without papers or permission.

So my sweetheart, let's bid farewell
again to customary pressures,
my companion-in-life, dear-heart!, lover: us.

I'll Tell You a Story, So I Can Ride My Horse in Peace

Once upon a time a forty-year old
man named Giovanni met a like-aged
woman with blonde hair, who managed a café.
They courted months before he brought her home
to meet Mama. Anxious to please, the girlfriend
enlisted Maria Perego, the seventy-year old lady
who baked *biscotti* for the café. All day long
her sauce simmered, and Maria was proud
to share recipes with this pretty,
but wholly-inept-in-the-kitchen young
woman trying to impress--*impossible*--an Italian mother.

With the canteen of sauce in her arms,
Italian greetings in her mouth,
the blonde woman enters the house with *Ciao*!
hello! *come sta*? on her lips
to which the old lady, dressed in black,
mumbles inaudibly and throws
curry in the rice. Months later,
Giovanni, now John, admitted
to being Abdul, telling the story
of his college years when he was beaten
by white boys who hated Iranians.
He changed his name, passed for Italian.
But not Mama. Never Mama.

* * * * *

On my walking route, a beautiful blonde
woman rides bare back on a grey-white

horse. They trot past me, we say hello.
Ethnicity, ethnicity, how pretty
you are: we ride together daily
on cobblestone roads--clomp, clomp, clomp,
you go, like the beating of my heart.

ABOUT THE AUTHOR

MARY JO BONA is the author of *By the Breath of Their Mouths: Narratives of Resistance in Italian America*; *Claiming a Tradition: Italian American Women Writers*; editor of *The Voices We Carry: Recent Italian American Women's Fiction*; and co-editor of *Multiethnic Literature and Canon Debates*. She was guest editor of MELUS (Multiethnic Literature of the United States) on Italian American literature. Bona is also series editor of Multiethnic Literature at SUNY Press. She has completed a manuscript that examines representations of migratory women through the trope of needlework.

Professor Bona received a stipendiary award and entrance into the Academy of Teacher Scholars at Stony Brook and was a recipient of the Elena Lucrezia Cornaro award for significant contributions to her profession and community. She is a member of the Department of Cultural Analysis and Theory; she also teaches both literature and cultural courses for European Languages, English, and Women's and Gender Studies. Such courses include Italian American and African American Women Writers, Italian Americans and Ethnic Relations, Images of Women in Italian American Culture and Italian American Film.

She served as president of AIHA, the American Italian Historical Association, and on the advisory committee of NIAF, the National Italian American Foundation. Professor Bona serves as an officer of MELUS, the association for the study of multiethnic literature of the United States. Professor Bona's scholarly interests are inclusive of Italian American literature and culture, and multiethnic and women's literature.

VIA FOLIOS
A refereed book series dedicated to the culture of Italians and Italian Americans.

Bordighera Press is an imprint of Bordighera, Incorporated, an independently owned not-for-profit scholarly organization that has no legal affiliation with the University of Central Florida or with The John D. Calandra Italian American Institute, Queens College/CUNY.

BASSETTI, ACCOLLA, D'AQUINO, *Italici: An Encounter with Piero Bassetti*, Vol. 55, Italian Studies, $8

GIOSE RIMANELLI, *The Three-legged One*, Vol. 54, Fiction, $15

CHARLES KLOPP, *Bele Antiche Stòrie*, Vol. 53, Criticism, $25

JOSEPH RICAPITO, *Second Wave*, Vol. 52, Poetry, $12

GARY MORMINO, *Italians in Florida*, Vol. 51, History, $15

GIANFRANCO ANGELUCCI, *Federico F.*, Vol. 50, Fiction, $15

ANTHONY VALERIO, *The Little Sailor*, Vol. 49, Memoir, $9

ROSS TALARICO, *The Reptilian Interludes*, Vol. 48, Poetry, $15

RACHEL GUIDO DE VRIES, *Teeny Tiny Tino's Fishing Story*, Vol. 47, Children's Literature, $6

EMANUEL DI PASQUALE, *Writing Anew*, Vol. 46, Poetry, $15

MARIA FAMÀ, *Looking For Cover*, Vol. 45, Poetry, $12

ANTHONY VALERIO, *Toni Cade Bambara's One Sicilian Night*, Vol. 44, Poetry, $10

EMANUEL CARNEVALI, Dennis Barone, Ed., *Furnished Rooms*, Vol. 43, Poetry, $14

BRENT ADKINS, et al., Ed., *Shifting Borders, Negotiating Places*, Vol. 42, Proceedings, $18

GEORGE GUIDA, *Low Italian*, Vol. 41, Poetry, $11

GARDAPHÈ, GIORDANO, TAMBURRI, *Introducing Italian Americana*, Vol. 40, Italian/American Studies, $10

DANIELA GIOSEFFI, *Blood Autumn/Autunno di sangue*, Vol. 39, Poetry, $15/$25

FRED MISURELLA, *Lies to Live by*, Vol. 38, Stories, $15

STEVEN BELLUSCIO, *Constructing a Bibliography*, Vol. 37, Italian Americana, $15

ANTHONY JULIAN TAMBURRI, Ed., *Italian Cultural Studies 2002*, Vol. 36, Essays, $18

BEA TUSIANI, *con amore*, Vol. 35, Memoir, $19

FLAVIA BRIZIO-SKOV, Ed., *Reconstructing Societies in the Aftermath of War*, Vol. 34, History, $30

TAMBURRI, et al., Eds., *Italian Cultural Studies 2001*, Vol. 33, Essays, $18

ELIZABETH G. MESSINA, Ed., *In Our Own Voices*, Vol. 32, Italian/American Studies, $25

STANISLAO G. PUGLIESE, *Desperate Inscriptions*, Vol. 31, History, $12

HOSTERT & TAMBURRI, Eds., *Screening Ethnicity*, Vol. 30, Italian/American Culture, $25

G. PARATI & B. LAWTON, Eds., *Italian Cultural Studies*, Vol. 29, Essays, $18

HELEN BAROLINI, *More Italian Hours*, Vol. 28, Fiction, $16

FRANCO NASI, Ed., *Intorno alla Via Emilia*, Vol. 27, Culture, $16

ARTHUR L. CLEMENTS, *The Book of Madness & Love*, Vol. 26, Poetry, $10

JOHN CASEY, et al., *Imagining Humanity*, Vol. 25, Interdisciplinary Studies, $18

ROBERT LIMA, *Sardinia/Sardegna*, Vol. 24, Poetry, $10

DANIELA GIOSEFFI, *Going On*, Vol. 23, Poetry, $10

ROSS TALARICO, *The Journey Home*, Vol. 22, Poetry, $12

EMANUEL DI PASQUALE, *The Silver Lake Love Poems*, Vol. 21, Poetry, $7

JOSEPH TUSIANI, *Ethnicity*, Vol. 20, Poetry, $12

JENNIFER LAGIER, *Second Class Citizen*, Vol. 19, Poetry, $8

FELIX STEFANILE, *The Country of Absence*, Vol. 18, Poetry, $9

PHILIP CANNISTRARO, *Blackshirts*, Vol. 17, History, $12

LUIGI RUSTICHELLI, Ed., *Seminario sul racconto*, Vol. 16, Narrative, $10

LEWIS TURCO, *Shaking the Family Tree*, Vol. 15, Memoirs, $9

LUIGI RUSTICHELLI, Ed., *Seminario sulla drammaturgia*, Vol. 14, Theater/Essays, $10

FRED GARDAPHÈ, *Moustache Pete is Dead! Long Live Moustache Pete!*, Vol. 13, Oral Literature, $10

JONE GAILLARD CORSI, *Il libretto d'autore, 1860–1930*, Vol. 12, Criticism, $17

HELEN BAROLINI, *Chiaroscuro: Essays of Identity*, Vol. 11, Essays, $15

PICARAZZI & FEINSTEIN, Eds., *An African Harlequin in Milan*, Vol. 10, Theater/Essays, $15

JOSEPH RICAPITO, *Florentine Streets & Other Poems*, Vol. 9, Poetry, $9